Susan, you are an amazing woman of God!!

...from the shadows and be seen. It's time to release your prophetic utterance. No more hiding. It's time to shine brightly

— Modelina [?]

Emerge

Intro: Emerging Nehemiah's

Chapter 1: Emerging in the Spirit

Chapter 2: Voice Recognition

Chapter 3: Born as Kings, Known as Servants

Chapter 4: Emerging Finances

Chapter 5: Emerging as a prophetic people

Copyright © 2017 by Johnathan Stidham

Emerge

It's your turn

Printed in the United States

IBSN 978-0692825419 (Johnathan Stidham Ministries)

All rights reserved by author. The author guarantees all content are original and do not infringe upon the legal rights of any person or work. No part of this book may be reproduced, stored in a retrieval system, or transmitted in any form or by any means without expressed written permission of the author.

Scripture quotations, unless other wise noted, are taken from the New American Standard Bible. Copyright © 1960, 1962, 1963, 1968, 1971, 1972, 1973,1975, 1977, 1995 by The Lockman Foundation.

JohnathanStidham.com

e·merge

come out, appear, come into view, become visible, surface, materialize, manifest oneself, issue, come forth

Johnathan Stidham
Madeline James

God has a natural response to chaos and darkness and that is to call light into being. As the light emerges and begins to spread, all darkness begins to dissipate. When God wants a new sound to bring forth His light or purpose, he emerges a new era. Their combative techniques are innovative, thus rendering their upgraded thought process more advanced than the enemy. There is an era emerging that is disenchanted with systems, functions, and the lack of power that is being displayed in the Body of Christ. They are hungry and willing to do what it takes to see the church look like the book of Acts once again. They have new concepts, dress differently, have a different spiritual vernacular, and are ready to wreck this world with the good news of Jesus Christ. Much like Joseph's, the dreams of this era will intimidate those who have been paralyzed by religion.

- Johnathan Stidham

Emerging Nehemiahs

There is an era emerging from out of the presence of God with a mandate to rebuild the ruins. They are clothed with power and moved by the love of the Father for people. They will stand before kings, and the glory will speak for them! Nehemiah loved his country. You cannot have authority over what you cannot love. Love is the ultimate expression of God. God's love transcends our natural mind and is beautifully balanced with truth and grace.

Nehemiah was a man of prayer. We are called to be people who steward the presence of God. We often fight battles in our own strength when we lack proper understanding of our identity as sons of God. The presence of God transformed Nehemiah to the point that the King noticed his countenance changed. Nehemiah's have a heart to express the fullness of God through their lives, by encountering God in the secret places, and being transformed into His image. They allow God to fight their battles, and trust Him for the proper outcome.

> *"There is an era emerging from out of the presence of God with a mandate to rebuild the ruins. They are clothed with power and moved by the love of the Father for people."*

When you begin building (working for the Lord) you must beware of the tactics that will come against you. Nehemiah 2:19 says:

> *"But when Sanballat, Tobiah, and Greshem the Arab heard of our plan, they scoffed contemptuously. 'What are you doing? Are you rebelling against the king?' they asked."*

*Sanballats: Area spirit of distraction, an enemy in the secret.

These are wolves in sheep's clothing. Sanballats were under the rule of the king, yet they hated him and Nehemiah. You must recognize your Judas. When God increases your influence in heaven and on earth, the devil will send people into your life with the intent to derail your future and snuff out your hope. You must be wise to the tactics of the enemy.   James 1:19 NASB:

> *"This you know, my beloved brethren. But everyone must be quick to hear, slow to speak and slow to anger."*

*Tobias : means "the Lord is good"

While you are building, you must be aware of when even the people you call family in the Lord have lost understanding and will no longer make the trip—for good people to be called out of your life to fulfill the mandate on their life as well. Good people can become enemies of your destiny. Many make separation a negative in every situation. We find in Acts 15 that separation became multiplication. Paul and Barnabas separate because of Mark, resulting in them both making more disciples and expanding the kingdom. Both Paul and Barnabas loved Jesus. They just had different assignments. The revelation they carried for their assignments began to make them war against each other.

> *"Good people can become enemies of your destiny."*

When I started in ministry, the Lord asked me to hold both of my hands parallel to the floor, palms to the sky, shoulder length apart. He then proceeded to tell me, "The right hand represented every person that would come in to my life, and the left hand represented people who would not stay in my life. The distance between my right and left hand represented my journey with everyone that would come into my life." The Lord told me that I would never be allowed to take ownership of people. Some would stay in my right hand the entirety of my life and never leave. Many more would journey to my left hand. Pain will cause you to clinch your hands into a fist and try to take ownership, ultimately leading to a spirit of control and manipulation.

This word changed my life. I realized that I have one shot to pour everything I have into those who would come into my life. Many good people would not make the entire journey. To hold them would not only stifle the spirit of God in my life, but would hinder their destiny as well.

*Geshem: means "rain storm"

You must know who your open enemies are. Identifying the demonic resistance against you will help direct your warfare. As you emerge, it will become important that you are able to identify the caliber of the demonic opposition you are facing and what strongholds reign in the region you have been assigned to. When my wife and I moved to Kentucky, we began to experience mental fatigue and racing thoughts. Because this was abnormal in our lives,

> *"As you emerge it will become important that you are able to identify the caliber of demonic opposition you are facing and what strongholds reign in the region you have been assigned to."*

I began to fast and pray for clarity. Within weeks, our intercessors began to have dreams and visions of a python coiled around this region. We immediately began to break the spirit of python and the fatigue and racing thoughts began to subside.

This Nehemiah generation is anointed to unlock generations that have been bound by unseen wounds, religion, and physical bondage. In Acts chapter 3, we find Peter and John going to the temple to pray. (This is a daily Jewish custom. We find in Luke 4:16 that Jesus went to the synagogue (church) as was his custom.) As Peter and John were traveling by foot to worship in the temple, they came across a man who had been lame (crippled) since birth. He was begging for money, and many before Peter and John gave out of sincere hearts, not having the power of Holy Spirit. The lame man received healing that day because Peter and John were heading to their appointed place. This gave them opportunity to preach about Jesus! Being in your appointed place leads to divine encounters, which provide places for you to talk about Jesus.

God is bringing forth those who understand the value of assignment. They are not moved by adversity, and will not be moved by opportunities that are void of His presence. This era places weight on being at their appointed place, insuring that the

Kingdom of God is advancing. Many will be unlocked and unshackled from their current circumstances.

Discernment and Wisdom

Discernment will be your greatest weapon in this next era as you emerge. Discernment allows you to know what is true, and what is not. It enables you to know the source from which a person is operating in. Discernment is not something that can be taught, it's a knowing. Like Nehemiah, once you begin to spend time in the secret place, the Holy Spirit will grow and nurture the gift of discernment within. You do not want to be caught without discernment in your arsenal.

Discernment is key for you to know how to point out the Sanballots, Tobias', and Geshem's in your life. Discernment also enables you to see beyond the surface, into the heart of those around you. The deception and hidden motives of the enemy are at an all-time high. Without discernment, we are left open to hidden attacks from the enemy. Discernment allows you to know what you are dealing with. As we advance the Kingdom in this hour, we cannot go in blindly. We must know and discern what will come against us.

Wisdom and discernment are the secret weapons the enemy doesn't want you to have or utilize. Wisdom is the ability to apply the counsel of God to your knowledge, insight, and understanding. It helps you choose the best course of action. Nehemiah was able to gain wisdom and discernment as he spent time in the secret place. The instructions for your assignments will come from time spent in the secret place.

You will need greater wisdom in this next era to build the ruins of your generation. If you lack wisdom, the word of God says to ask for it and God will give it to you. (James 1:5). In this next era, precision and intentionality will be important. We cannot rebuild the ruins in a flippant manner. There must be honor, and purpose in what we build. There is no time to waste. It's time to rebuild, and advance the Kingdom of God.

> *"As we advance the Kingdom in this hour, we cannot go in blindly. We must know and discern what will come against us."*

Emerging in the Spirit

Isaiah 11:1-3 (NASB)

"Then a shoot will spring from the stem of Jesse, And a branch from his roots will bear fruit. The Spirit of the LORD will rest on Him, The spirit of wisdom and understanding, The spirit of counsel and strength, The spirit of knowledge and the fear of the LORD. And He will delight in the fear of the LORD."

Galatians 5:22-23 (NASB)

"But the fruit of the Spirit is love, joy, peace, patience, kindness, goodness, faithfulness, gentleness, self-control; against such things there is no law."

1 Corinthians 12:8-11 (NASB)

"For to one is given the word of wisdom through the Spirit, and to another the word of knowledge according to the same Spirit; to another faith by the same Spirit, and to another gifts of healing by the one Spirit, and to another the effecting of miracles, and to another prophecy, and to another the distinguishing of spirits, to another various kinds of tongues, and to another the interpretation of tongues. But one and the same Spirit works all these things, distributing to each one individually just as He wills."

Wisdom

But by His doing, you are in Christ Jesus, who became to us wisdom from God, and righteousness and sanctification, and redemption

-1 Corinthians 1:30 NASB

As believers we must have a sound understanding of who we are in Christ and how to travel in the spiritual vehicle of wisdom. We read in Proverbs 8:22 that the Lord possessed wisdom from the very beginning. Wisdom is a virtue of the Holy Spirit found in Isaiah 11:1-3. We also find these seven virtues found before the throne of God in Revelation 5:6. It is important to know there are not seven Holy Spirits but rather seven complete and perfect virtues or characteristics of Him. So before time was ever thought of the God who is eternity and created eternity, the council of God, convened, and the archangels recorded their conversation. In the council of God is, the Father, the Word, and the Holy Ghost. So when

> *"As believers we must have a sound understanding of who we are in Christ and how to travel in the spiritual vehicle of wisdom."*
>
> *–Johnathan Stidham*

Gabriel in John 1 came to Elizabeth and Mary, he gave them a glimpse of the eternal, or real, when he makes the statement, "I am the angel who stands in the presence of God." It was there that the plan for all of humanity was laid out and the fall of man was foreseen, even though it had never happened. The willing decision by the Word was made to become human and be the lamb slain before the foundation of the earth (1 Peter 1:20 NASB)

Wisdom is the spiritual conduit that God uses for us to move and operate within the spirit realm. It is our gift from God to be able to see into situations before they happen, to maneuver around obstacles from the vantage point of Heaven, to see into what is going to be, and calling it into our present and allowing us to walk presently in a blessing that was laid up for later.

> *Wisdom is the spiritual conduit that God uses for us to move and operate within the spirit realm.*
>
> *–Johnathan Stidham*

Proverbs 8:22 says." the Lord possessed wisdom from the beginning." This is a prophetic passage pointing to the Risen Lord Jesus Christ before the Word had become flesh and died on the cross. When Jesus was born, Revelation 12:5 says that he was caught up with God. The remainder of that chapter is about a dragon (the devil) that came to kill Jesus. Wisdom saw this attack before it was conceived in the mind of Lucifer, and already had a strategic plan in place. Though Jesus was on earth, he was hidden by heaven because it was not his time to die.

The Council of God

When the council of God looked into the span of time to the very moment in which Adam and Eve would fall, the justice of God began to speak into the situation and demanded that something be done to vindicate God's sovereignty. This is much like Genesis chapter 6 declaring that Noah was a righteous man who walked with God. The earth, however, was wicked and God was going to destroy it all. The Lord utilized wisdom and decided to spare a righteous family and have them fill the earth with their seed, prophetically allowing us to see the strength of His covenant with the seed. So as justice finished speaking, wisdom began to speak about the blood of an innocent man being shed that would break the curse of sin on humanity—that through the blood of Jesus we would be grafted into Christ and would rule and reign again on earth. Anything coming into the hands of the righteous would be redeemed. The plan was drafted, commissioned and carried out. Jesus would become wisdom, and we would be in Christ having the ability to apprehend the very wisdom of God (James 1:5 NASB.) The plan of wisdom that was drafted was revealed in Matthew 10:8. Heal the sick, raise the dead, cleanse the lepers, cast out demons. Freely you received, freely give. It was set that as sons and daughters we would be commissioned with all power and authority to govern the earth.

Jurisdiction and Authority

As believers, we operate from three heavens of jurisdiction. All three realms are co-equal in creation and cooperative in function with one another, just as God was, is, and will always be. As the Godhead encompasses the Father, Son, and Holy Ghost we were also made in the three dimensions of body, soul, and spirit. We operate in three realms as well; Revelation, Character and Anointing. There must be equal influences placed on all three realms; to be absent of one is to be off-balanced in all. Jesus lived this model for us as an example.

When Jesus spoke to the Jewish people trying to kill him in John 5 he tells them *"he only does what he sees the Father do, and says what hears Father has spoken."* He was operating in the realm of eternal revelation. This is where the plans of God have been spoken in the council of God.

In Acts 19:15 we read about Jewish priests who were trying to operate in the second heaven, or unseen world without a relationship with Jesus and the absence of power in the Holy Ghost. They tried to cast out a demon and the seven sons of Sceva spoke up and said, "Jesus I know, Paul I know, but who are you?" Paul gives another account of the second heavens in Ephesians 6:12. These are a couple of passages that give insight to the Gifts of the spirit operating in the unseen realm or second heaven.

We have many account of Jesus operating in the physical realm or first heaven, displaying the fruits of the spirit. From washing the disciple feet, feeding the hungry, and showing compassion for the sick. The key to manifesting the right fruit and unlocking authority on earth is having a proper understanding of identity in Christ—that we are seated in heavenly places. We become detrimental when our revelation of who God

> *"We become detrimental when our revelation of whom God is, and the understanding of whom God has called us be. Do not manifest into a lifestyles that attracts others to Jesus."*
>
> *–Johnathan Stidham*

is and the understanding of who God has called us be does not manifest into a lifestyles that attracts others to Jesus.

1st Heaven

"But the fruit of the Spirit is love, joy, peace, patience, kindness, goodness, faithfulness, gentleness, self-control; against such things there is no law."

Galatians 5:22-23 (NASB)

The atmospheric heaven encompasses all that we see and the air that we breathe. *"I will destroy humanity whom I have created from the face of the earth, humans and beasts, creeping thing and birds of heaven."* (Genesis 6:7.) When God formed man he gave him dominion authority over the first heaven. This is seen in Genesis 1:26 (NASB):

"Then God said, 'Let Us make man in Our image, according to Our likeness; and let them rule over the fish of the sea and over the birds of the sky and over the cattle and over all the earth, and over every creeping thing that creeps on the earth."

It was always God's desire for his sons and daughters to have complete reign on earth. When the fall of man happened because of sin, humanity lost its authority in the 1st heaven. The bible declares that Jesus came to seek and save that which was lost. He would not only reconcile us into relationship and right standing, but restore dominion authority over all of the earth as well. The earth is mourning for sons and daughters to come into the understanding of sonship and begin to walk in the fruits of the Spirit as well as the power of the Spirit.

In the first heaven there are two manifestation of Holy Spirit that takes place in the life of a believer. Salvation, which produces the fruits of the spirit and the Baptism of the Holy Spirit, produces His power. When a person gives their life to Jesus, Holy Spirit comes in and makes residence inside of them. In Galatians 4 the bible declares that you are no longer slaves but heirs as sons. When you come into Christ your spirit is awakened and married to Holy Spirit. You become one, covered in the shadow of the almighty. That's why the Bible goes on to say that your body is the temple of the Holy Ghost. The process of sanctification is your soul becoming what the blood of Jesus says you are when you get saved. This process is a journey over the entirety of our life, but our spirit is immediately made one with Holy Spirit and seated in heavenly places with Jesus.

The fruits of the spirit have two functions; to allow the world to see Jesus through your life—the fruits of the Spirit are God manifesting proof that Holy Spirit has awakened your spirit and made his home inside of you, and to let the spirit realm know that you have rights to the inheritance you will be occupying as a son or daughter here on earth.

As believers, we have been given all power and authority in Jesus Christ. When Jesus died, he commissioned us as believers to go and retrieve it for him, to win the lost, cast out demons, heal the sick, and raise the dead. God has called us to govern all of the first heaven for Him, including economy, buildings, land, government, social media, education, entertainment, and business. In Genesis 2:4 and Genesis 2:7 we find that there is a difference in all God created (heaven and earth) and all God formed (humanity.) As we begin to inhabit all God created we must have the fruit of the Spirit on display as an indicator that we have the right to move in the authority of Christ. The fruits of the Spirit are the title deed in the spirit realm that you are a child of God and his inheritance has become your Inheritance.

Second Heaven

"For we wrestle not against flesh and blood, but against principalities, against powers, against the rulers of the darkness of this world, against spiritual wickedness in high places."

-Ephesians 6:12 (KJV)

"But the prince of the kingdom of Persia was withstanding me for twenty-one days; then behold, Michael, one of the chief princes, came to help me, for I had been left there with the kings of Persia." - Daniel 10:13 (NASB)

Emerging in the spirit must come with a sound understanding of the structure and warfare of the second heavens. As God, the Word, and Holy Spirit convened in the council of heaven, the archangels stood in the presence of God including Lucifer. As the plan for humanity began to unfold (God would create

> *"Power is the ability to do something or act in a certain way. Authority is your right to operate in the power in which you are demonstrating."*
>
> *– Johnathan Stidham*

humanity to worship and fellowship with Him), thoughts built up in the mind of Lucifer, and he conceived a thought: "He would be like the Most High God." (Isaiah 14:12-15 NASB) It was then that Lucifer was smacked out of heaven and fell like a bolt of lightning. We pick up the battle in Revelation 12, where a war raged in the second heaven of demonic principalities against angelic principalities. In verse 8 the bible says there was no longer a place for Satan in heaven. This is the third heaven where God abides.

We must know that Satan is not omnipresent. He and all other demons must have a place or person to abide in to maintain position or manifest in the first heaven. If not, they must go back to the second heaven as strongholds. God is able to fill the earth with His presence, to live in Jesus yet be in heaven at the same time, to fill everyone who accepts him, and be upon everyone who receives the baptism of the Holy Spirit. The moment there was not a place for Satan, he set out to find refuge in the things God created and formed. When the fall of humanity took place, Satan began to implement his kingdom as he heard God would in the council at the very beginning. There remained one problem, Satan also heard the answer to the problem of humanity falling. God would come as man, live a sinless life, be crucified, be raised from the dead 3 days later, and be seated in glory at the right hand of God. That moment would lead humanity to receive the Spirit of God through salvation and the power to destroy the kingdom of darkness. From Genesis to the book of John you will read of attempts by Satan to destroy people and lineage. The enemy's hope would be that someone, through sin would abort the plan of God.

For the enemy to operate legally, he must have a place to abide. *"This is the account of the heavens and the earth when they were created, in the day that the LORD God made earth and heaven."* (Genesis 2:4 NASB) Why is the devil after the systems of the world? We find the answer in Romans 1:20—all of creation gives God glory. Because structures and systems of the world are not living organisms, the enemy will occupy them by strongholds establishing gates in the spirit. Literally in the spirit the devil will occupy economy, businesses, buildings, or land by erecting a throne in the spirit and empowering a demonic principality to govern what has been taken hostage. As long as a demonic principality has dominion over that occupied place there is a false glory that will manifest for Satan. When Peter confessed that Jesus was Christ, the son of the living God, Jesus responds by declaring that upon that revelation God would build his church and the gates of hell would not prevail.

The ultimate goal of the devil is to possess the unbeliever and oppress believers.

> *"Then the LORD God formed man of dust from the ground, and breathed into his nostrils the breath of life; and man became a living being."*
>
> -Genesis 2:7 NASB

All of humanity was created with a future and hope. Your life was designed to be a sweet fragrance of worship to God. Paul brought forth a profound passage when he said we do not fight against flesh and blood, but principalities.

It is important that we discern the spirit that is in operation behind the person or situation that we encounter. We were designed in Christ to war in the second heavens. We are called to tear down the strongholds of the enemy and to rebuke the spirits in operation behind the behavior of people. In the second heaven we are not fighting for victory, we are fighting from a place of victory. We are to pull down the strongholds and occupy them ourselves in the spirit. The devil will always try to make your fight in the soul realm because that is his jurisdiction. Every time a believer takes the fight into the spirit realm and addresses the principalities that are at work, they walk in the authority of Christ.

In Daniel chapter 10 we see that as Daniel prayed an angel was commissioned to him, but the angel was caught in a fight with a demonic principality. After the archangel Gabriel came to the rescue, the angel appears to Daniel who was still steadfast in prayer. His angel let him know that on the first day of prayer God heard him and he had been commissioned to Daniel. Jesus walks up to the tomb of Lazarus and opens his prayer with, "Father I know you always here me." It is imperative that you know God has heard your prayers. He is not ignoring you. Angels were commissioned to carry out the good and perfect will of God for you. When they leave the third heaven, angels encounter fights by the strongholds in the second heaven. As believers we must stand in the authority of Christ and come against these wicked strongholds so the angels that minister God's will can be free to carry our their task.

> *"Truly I say to you, whatever you bind on earth shall have been bound in heaven; and whatever you loose on earth shall have been loosed in heaven."*
>
> Matthew 18:18 NASB

Weapons of Our Warfare

We must to continue to remind ourselves we are fighting a spiritual battle. Many times we wear ourselves out because we are fighting in the wrong manner or realm. We must remember we are spirit first, then man. Our warfare has to be intentional and direct. Paul tells us in 1 Corinthians 9:26, *"Therefore I do not run like someone running aimlessly; I do not fight like a boxer beating the air.*" Any time we go into battle it's imperative to access the council of God. When we draw from the wisdom and counsel of the Lord and apply it, victory is ensured. If we don't ask the Lord for His insight and wisdom we'll be beating the air and running aimlessly like Paul said. Your greatest partner in engaging in warfare is partnering with the Holy Spirit.

Warfare can become overwhelming and open us up to being hit when we engage in battles the Lord has not authorized us to fight in. The Lord doesn't lead us into a battle to lose. The Word of God tells us, "*He leads us in triumph and victory*" (2 Corinthians 2:14). Make note, the Word says He leads us. The Spirit will never lead you into a battle to cause you to fail. Defeat happens when we step out of the leading and protection of Holy Spirit. As you emerge, each level will require the leading and approach of the Spirit in a greater measure. He has already gone before us and knows the strategy needed to fight in this season or level.

As stated previously throughout this chapter, "We are not fighting against flesh-and-blood enemies, but against evil rulers and authorities of the unseen world, against evil rulers and mighty powers in this dark world, and against evil spirits in the heavenly places (Ephesians 6:12). Often times we go into warfare using human reasoning and logic when God has given us spiritual weapons to fight with. You cannot fight the spiritual with the carnal. 2 Corinthians 10:4-5 declares:

"The weapons we fight with are not the weapons of the world. On contrary, they have divine power to demolish strongholds. We demolish arguments and every pretention that sets itself up against the knowledge of God."

Paul also tells us before going into battle to put on the full armor of God (Ephesians 6:13).

When God created the heavens, He established the hierarchies of the heavens. When Lucifer fell, He established counterfeit hierarchies as we see listed in Ephesians 6:12. When we are able to understand how the spirit realm is ordered and how it functions, we will have success in our warfare. We'll know what to address in a person or region. The enemy establishes strongholds and dominions over regions and people when he is given legal access. Strongholds and authorities can be overthrown and taken down when we use the strategies of heaven because they carry divine power.

We're in a time where old methods of warfare and strategies are not working or having the impact they once had. Paul encourages us to pray in the Spirit at times and on every occasion (Ephesians 6:18). When we pray in the Spirit, it gives us access to the council of God and access to the Lord's armory (Jeremiah 50:25). As a prophetic and Spirit led people, we must wage war prophetically. It's time to exchange old methods, strategies, and weapons. God is releasing a new era which requires us to battle in a new way.

Voice Recognition

In the beginning was the Word, and the Word was with God, and the Word was God.

–John 1:1 KJV

And God said, Let there be light: and there was light. And God saw the light, that it was good: and God divided the light from the darkness.

–Genesis 1:3-4 KJV

Everything God created, came from who God is. John 1:3 says, "All things were made by him; and without him was not anything made that was made. In Genesis 1, God spoke everything into being. From that, we are able to realize God placed great emphasis on voice recognition.

> **"Often times we desire for our voice to emerge in a generation, without the understanding of the importance of character."**

Often times we desire for our voice to emerge in a generation without the understanding of the importance of character. Everything God does is in divine order and in an established pattern

His children can follow. Your voice carries such power and authority. When we don't have proper understanding of our identity in Christ and character, it can lead to disaster. The voice intended to partner with heaven, to bring forth God's plans can unknowingly partner with hell to bring forth the agenda of the devil if we don't carry the proper character.

Your voice is a trumpet recognized in heaven and echoed throughout the earth. Your voice emerges from a place of identity in Christ. We look to the story of Adam and Eve and realized that Eve did not receive her name until after the fall. Genesis 3:20 states, *"And Adam called his wife's name Eve; because she was the mother of all living."* Often times we relegate our identity with who we used to be and not who we are in Christ. Part of your voice emerging is connected to the understanding of who you are in Christ. As sons and daughters of God, we must come to the realization and understanding that we are seated in high places with Jesus. We are a royal priesthood, a chosen generation. (1 Peter 2:9). This understanding of sonship is imperative as you discover the

> *"Your voice is a trumpet that is recognized in heaven and echoed throughout the earth."*
>
> *-Johnathan Stidham*

authority in your voice. God, who is the first seer, created everything by His voice. In Genesis 1, when God spoke He spoke from a place of being. Everything was created from the identity of who God is. After He spoke those things into existence, God said it was good to His sight (Genesis 1:31).

As God begins to reveal you to the world, the last thing to emerge will be your voice. Don't get frustrated; many will notice you long before they hear you. The emerging process is ordained by heaven. The disciples walked with Jesus for two years before their voice emerged as leaders. In John 18:15-17, Peter is in the courtyard after Jesus had been taken into custody. The Bible tells us the people noticed who Peter was, a follower of Jesus. In that moment Peter used his voice to deny Jesus, but later we read Jesus restored Peter. In Acts 2 his voice emerges.

In the book of Acts chapter 2, the spirit of God comes upon the believers on the day of Pentecost. Peter emerges as the spokesman to the public. When he began to speak to the crowd, they were captivated by his knowledge of the word and the authority in which he spoke. What was different? Peter was restored by Jesus. His voice carried the weight of the encounter, but his boldness came from a place

> *"Peters voice carried the weight of the encounter, but his boldness came from a place of identity."*

of identity. The culmination of both caused his voice to carry the influence of Heaven while he spoke the words of the Lord.

Peter's Voice

> *And as Peter knocked at the door of the gate, a damsel came to hearken, named Rhoda. And when she knew Peter's voice, she opened not the gate for gladness, but ran in, and told how Peter stood before the gate.* –Acts 12:13-14 KJV

In Acts chapter 12, Peter found himself locked up in prison. The Bible says an angel of the Lord came and shook the prison. The gates opened up, and Peter was released. Then the angel of the Lord led Peter to the house where the disciples were staying. When Peter gets to the house he knocks on the door. A servant named Rhoda recognizes the voice of Peter, and runs to the disciples to tell them, *"Peter is here"* (Acts 12:14). The Disciples believed she was crazy and said, "I*t must be the angel of Peter"* (Acts 12:15). But Peter knocked again. When he spoke, the disciples came to open the door, and there stood Peter.

If we're not careful, we can bypass this passage, and fail to realize the significance of Rhoda recognizing the voice of Peter. What is taking place in the spirit realm through your consistent prayer life is that your voice is being recorded in heaven. Rhoda is a beautiful depiction of angels that are assigned to doors, and opportunities in your life that recognize your voice. When it's your time to walk through doors, the places and opportunities that were closed off in your prior season will open with ease in this season. The systems of the world were uniquely patterned after the systems of heaven.

Your Voice

When God created you, before the foundations of the earth, He instilled the DNA of heaven within you. Psalm 139:15-16 says:

> *"My frame was not hidden from you when I was made in the secret place, when I was woven together in the depths of the earth. Your eyes saw my unformed body; all the days ordained for me were written in your book."*

As the Father began to form and fashion you in the secret place, He wove heaven's DNA into every fiber of your being. Nothing or no one can alter what's been placed within you. What was written in your book was made to correlate with what the Father placed inside of you.

The process of emerging enables us to discover our voice, and the things we are called to unlock. Everyone's voice is not called to unlock the same doors. When you find your voice and begin to release it, you'll notice your surroundings will begin to shift and move around you. Your voice is being recognized in the spirit realm. It's activates what's been dormant and unlocks what's been closed off.

Your voice not only unlocks, it carries a breaker anointing that enables an entire generation to inhabit their promise. In the book of Joshua, in the sixth chapter, we see all of Israel walking around Jericho. Many things stood in the way of them inhabiting what God had promised them, but God instructed them to march and say nothing until the seventh day. On the seventh day, the seventh time they walked around the city they were to blow the trumpets and lift up their voices and shout. Isaiah 58:1 declares, *"Cry aloud, spare not, lift up thy voice like a trumpet."* Our voices are the trumpet. Many are in bondage waiting for the walls to crumble so they can experience the promise of life, hope, blessings, freedom, relationship, love, joy, peace, and more. When you sound your voice, it causes the walls to crumble, and enable others to rightfully inhabit what God has for them.

Your words will carry an official order issued by a legal authority. Mathew 18:18 tells us:

> *"Verily I say unto you, whatsoever ye shall bind on earth shall be bound in heaven: and*

whatsoever ye shall loose on earth shall be loosed in heaven."

As a born again believer, you have the power to bind and loose with the power of Holy Spirit. But as your voice begins to emerge, there is a grace that comes upon your decree. That grace is called influence. The Lord begins to enlarge your borders, carrying the weight to unlock regions and nations.

Authority

> *"Authority is not found in someone's shout or scream, but in relationship with the Father."*

As God begins to emerge your voice to unlock things, your voice will begin to carry the authority of heaven. As God continues to process you and mold your character, He will add weight to your voice. Many in this season are walking in a false authority, and we've failed to recognize it. Authority is not found in someone's shout or scream, but in relationship with the Father. Your proximity to the Father will be reflected in your voice. The more we stay close to the Father, the more we become like Him and sound like Him (2 Corinthians 3:18).

There will be those who emerge alongside you that are carrying a counterfeit authority. Many will do things in the "name of the Lord" but will have no relationship. It's important to be discerning who you allow to speak into your life and who you run with. The spirit realm knows who walks in the true authority of Jesus Christ. We see an example of this in Acts 19. The Seven sons of Sceva were going around driving out demons in the name of Jesus. When they came to one particular person, the demon in them spoke out saying, "Jesus I know, and Paul I know, but who are you?" The sons of Sceva walked in a form of authority, but not the authority of Jesus Christ.

When God emerges you, the spirit realm will know your voice and the authority it carries. The authority you carry will cause you to be respected and demons will flee at the sound of your voice. In order to shift atmospheres, regions, and nations around you, your voice must bear the authority of heaven. If you don't allow the Lord to emerge you, you'll step in jurisdictions you have no authority to walk in. The sons of Sceva did just that, and opened the door for the enemy to come into their lives. When we step into matrons or jurisdictions we have no authority in, we experience warfare we're not equipped to battle in. Be led by the Spirit. He always leads us in triumph.

Born as Kings Known as Servants

"For thus says the LORD, "To the eunuchs who keep My Sabbaths, And choose what pleases Me, And hold fast My covenant, To them I will give in My house and within My walls a memorial, And a name better than that of sons and daughters; I will give them an everlasting name which will not be cut off.

-Isaiah 56:4-5 (NASB)

"Therefore Jesus answered and was saying to them, "Truly, truly, I say to you, the Son can do nothing of Himself, unless it is something He sees the Father doing; for whatever the Father does, these things the Son also does in like manner."

-John 5:19 (NASB)

"For even the Son of Man did not come to be served, but to serve, and to give His life a ransom for many."

-Mark 10:45 (NASB)

"Have this attitude in yourselves which was also in Christ Jesus, who, although He existed in the form of God, did not regard equality with God a thing to be grasped, but emptied Himself, taking the form of a bond-servant, and being made in the likeness of men. Being found in appearance as a

> *man, He humbled Himself by becoming obedient to the point of death, even death on a cross. For this reason also, God highly exalted Him, and bestowed on Him the name, which is above every name."*
>
> -Philippians 2:5-9 (NASB)

One of the greatest battles in the Kingdom of God is in the area of servant hood. This is an attack on the very nature of God to prevent the people of God from looking like Jesus. Every season of your emerging process will begin by the Lord asking you to go low. Your ability to submit to a man or woman of God will result in greater influence, jurisdiction, and authority in heaven and on earth. Why? The anointing of God flows from a place of humility and love. Often times our anointing is corrupted by bad doctrine, ideals, and mistakes that are preventable. All of them lead to hurt and frustration, which can be avoided by having the proper alignment and covering in our lives.

After the baptism and wilderness experience of Jesus, He emerges onto the scene empowered by the Holy Spirit. The Holy Spirit enables Him to live a life of servant hood, inspiration to us all. We read passages of Jesus washing the feet of his disciples, healing on the Sabbath, feeding the multitudes, and seeing the complete surrender of His will as He prayed in the garden of Gethsemane (Matthew 26:36-39.) Jesus was able to become of no reputation, living life as a servant to the plans of God. Because of this, His name was exalted to the highest place in heaven. The reward of servants leads to greater realms of influence in the heavens.

All believers become sons by adoption through Christ. However, not all sons become servants. Jesus, who was God, counted Himself not as equal to God but lowered himself (Philippians 2:6.) Jesus was the Word before He became flesh and God told his mother, Mary that he would be called Jesus (Luke 1:26-31.) The name Jesus was exalted because of His submission to the Father even unto death.

> *"Your ability to submit to a man or woman of God will result in greater influence, jurisdiction, and authority in heaven and on earth."*

Servant-hood

A life of servant hood does not devalue you as royal-priest; in fact it is quite the opposite. A person can never handle being in authority until they learn to be under authority. As you begin to emerge, it will be tempting to uproot from the posture of servant hood. If we are unable to stay in a posture of serving, we eliminate a significant part of our inheritance. An inheritance is given to sons through their fathers. Malachi 4:6 says, "*He will restore the hearts of the fathers to their children and the hearts of the children to their fathers.*"

Elisha: The Hand Washer

> *"We cannot afford for our sons and daughter to graduate from places that Jesus did not graduate from. Jesus came to serve and not to be served."*

If you are there when I leave, you can have my mantle. These are the words from Elijah to Elisha. Elijah, was not only God's prophet, he was a father. We can easily conclude because of the gifting on Elisha's life and training with Elijah, he was going to be a strong prophet. Elisha served Elijah as his hand washer for many years, being around his anointing and being trained prophetically. That was not enough for Elisha; he was determined to walk in a double portion anointing. Elijah knew in order for Elisha to continue the work of his spiritual father in a greater measure, Elisha could not afford to break his posture of servant hood.

Servant hood is not something you do; it is who you become. Elijah placed a demand on Elisha's request that he must be with him when God takes him to heaven. Fathers, do not hesitate to put a demand on your sons and daughters.

Nehemiah: The Cup Bearer

Burdened for his people and nation, Nehemiah begins to pray for favor with the Kings of the Persian Empire. He prayed for God to show the king the importance of him going to Jerusalem, and rebuilding the city (Nehemiah 1:11). How did Nehemiah, a Jew, gain access to the king of a Persian empire? It's important to note because Nehemiah served the king closely and well, King Cyrus noticed the countenance change of Nehemiah. Nehemiah was a faithful servant of King Cyrus. He loved God and loved the kings. Nehemiah's faithfulness to serve the king gave him favor in a position that was not usually favorable to a Jewish man.

Nehemiah was granted access to the ear of the kings. He stood before them, allowing the favor of God to work on his behalf.

Servants not only have the ear of the kings, they are the keeper of the kings' secrets. God elevates servants, and entrust them with His plans to bring about major changes throughout the world.

In the book of Esther, we find another example of the importance of having the king's ear. During this time period, King Xerxes decreed it was time to pick a queen. After Esther endured many months of grooming the king's eunuch (servant) comes into Esther's room to tell her it is time to stand before the king. As she goes to pick her clothes out, she asked the servant what he thinks she should wear before the king. The servant tells Esther what the king likes, and God's will was brought forth. Esther gained favor and was selected to be the queen who would later save the Jewish people from a major attack.

Because Nehemiah was a submitted man, the most powerful king of his time gave him a seal of authority. This authority granted Nehemiah accesses not only to rebuild God's city, but to pass through foreign regions without opposition. The power of a covering grants you the ability to build and labor in your calling, while covering you from major opposition and warfare that can take you out along your journey.

> *"God elevates servants, and entrust them with his plans to bring about major changes throughout the world."*

Paul: The Bondservant

Paul could have opened the book of Romans with many different titles that would've been noble and acceptable when describing the function of himself to the body of Christ. As we read, Paul describes himself as a servant. Paul was a man who understood the power of a submitted life! One major lesson we learn from Paul's life is a submitted life will require you to walk in hard places and through hard times. Although it may be difficult, there is always purpose in your journey.

In Acts 28, Paul is on his way to Rome when the ship he is aboard wrecks and they are washed up on the shore of an island called Malta. Now many would say this is a horrendous circumstance that they would never want to be apart of. This is not the mindset of a sold-out servant. There is purpose in the journey. By the time they are ready to leave, all of the sick on the island are healed. All that Paul needed, in Rome was furnished by the chief of the tribe in Malta.

As you learn to posture your heart in servant hood many things will happen, and be required out of you. The lesson I have learned in this journey is to fall in love with the process. God will always bring things full circle. Don't get caught up in the sacrifice, and lose sight of what God is doing in your heart along the way. No one was there to give Paul a pat on the back and say good job. This process should be filled with the heart to become more like Jesus.

Motives

Servant hood is the place where your motives die, so the King's agenda can go forth. Jesus said in Luke 9:23, *"Those who want to come with me must say no to the things they want, pick up their crosses every day, follow me."* (GWT) Serving is the process where the Father purifies our motives. When we go into serving others with hidden motives, the Lord will eventually expose them. He will not tolerate pride or hidden agendas.

In this day and age, many have gone into serving others with impure motives. They see mainstream men and women of God as an opportunity to use their platform for their own gain instead of being a gift to them. Many feel a sense of entitlement and believe they don't need to go through the process before the platform. The Father will not trust His secrets with those who try to bypass the process of serving. Before God is willing to elevate anyone in His Kingdom, He wants to know He can trust you with His name.

Serving is not always an act, but sometimes the posture of your heart. Jesus painted a beautiful picture of servant hood and humility in John 13 when he washed the disciples' feet. He said:

"I have set you an example that you should do as I have done for you. Very truly I tell you, no servant is greater than his master, nor is the messenger greater than the one who sent him."

-John 13:15-16

In the Kingdom of God, it's not about how high you can go. It's about how low are you willing to go. When you're willing to lay aside your agenda and your ambitions for the King's purposes, He knows he has found a trusted servant He can use. *"So humble yourselves under the mighty power of God, and at the right time he will lift you up in honor"* (1 Peter 5:6).

> ***"Serving is not always an act, but the posture of your heart."***

Emerging Finances

"When they came to Capernaum, those who collected the two-drachma tax came to Peter and said, 'Does your teacher not pay the two-drachma tax?' He said, 'Yes.' And when he came into the house, Jesus spoke to him first, saying, 'What do you think, Simon? From whom do the kings of the earth collect customs or poll-tax, from their sons or from strangers?' When Peter said, 'From strangers,' Jesus said to him, 'Then the sons are exempt. However, so that we do not offend them, go to the sea and throw in a hook, and take the first fish that comes up; and when you open its mouth, you will find a shekel. Take that and give it to them for you and Me."

Matthew 17:24-27 (NASB)

"But seek first His kingdom and His righteousness, and all these things will be added to you."

Matthew 6:33 (NASB)

A critical part of a believer's walk with the Lord is learning how to abound in much and little. This is a season and time where the Lord works on our character and passion for him rather than focus on the material things of the world. Unfortunately, part of the Body is stuck in learning and affirming how to live with little. Doctrines have been created to make people who prosper feel guilty for obtaining nice things. We can miss out on our influence and mandate to spread the Gospel, getting wrapped around a theology that restricts our thought process to lack or poverty (Ecclesiastes 10:19 KJV *but money answereth all things*).

There is a supernatural breakthrough that takes place as you emerge and step into your assignment from the Lord. In the Kingdom of God there is an importance of the alignment of seasons and timing under the heavens (Ecclesiastes 3:1). In this present time, we are living in a kiaros moment. Kiaros is a now moment where circumstances have come to a head to initiate the next dimension of your destiny. You are walking under an open heaven. Everything that was established for your journey now begins to flow freely from heaven into your life. Provision will manifest as you recognize your kiaros moment, step in obedience, and trust in what God has called you to do.

David's Journey

The Prophet Samuel interrupts David's life with a word from God. God had chosen him to be king over Israel (1 Samuel 16). A word from the Lord will often disrupt your life, causing things that were still to be set in motion. It causes a ripple effect in your life, and in the lives around you. Once the word is spoken, things will never be the same. The very moment oil was poured over David's head, heaven declared him to be king.

David's emerging process was very extensive. Many times we know our season is upon us, but we must learn to wait on the timing of the Lord. If David would have forced his way into the palace declaring to Saul that he was the new king, his life would have been cut short. It's important to learn how to navigate what's been set in motion. Many times, in our enthusiasm and immaturity, we forfeit the promise because we step out too soon. There will always be a waiting period between the declaration of the promise, and fully emerging into it.

Since David was willing to wait for the timing of the Lord. Every step of his emerging process was, provided for by God. David's patience allowed grace and provision to follow him in every area of his life. Each victory in battle was already manifested before David stepped on to the field. Every financial need was provided, and God divinely orchestrated every relationship. God divinely and strategically planned all of his steps to take him from the shepherd field to the palace.

Moses' Obedience

Many times we paralyze ourselves in the beginning stages of our journey, due to the financial mindsets we operate in. Often we believe there needs to be an extreme amount of financial faith in order for God to move financially as we emerge. When Moses came to the red sea, he did not have sea-splitting faith. Moses had a staff raised in obedience. Moses' obedience enabled his faith and confidence to grow in God with each step he took.

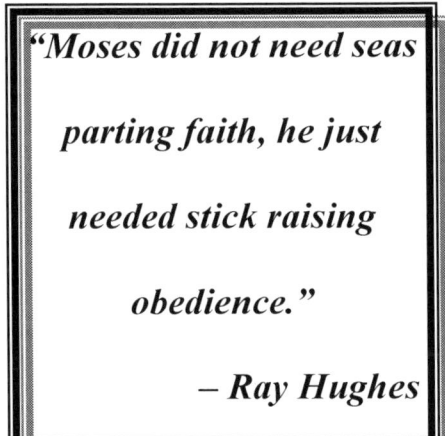

"Moses did not need seas parting faith, he just needed stick raising obedience."

– Ray Hughes

Many times the provision will not manifest until we take the first step. Our obedience sets things in motion. You must emerge with complete confidence in God's ability to take care of your journey. Paul stated this powerful truth he learned in his journey: *"And my God will supply all your needs according to*

His riches in glory in Christ Jesus" (Philippians 4:19). Moses and Paul didn't allow their circumstances or lack of supply in the moment to keep them from moving forward. To emerge, we are people called to walk by faith and not by sight (2 Corinthians 5:7).

<u>No More Delay</u>

God ordains processes through established patterns of heaven. The enemy strategically plans "pattern interruptions" in your emerging seasons. I have spoken to many believers who knew their season and timing was at hand but resistance came in the financial arena. We see an example of this in Daniel chapter 10. An angel was commissioned to Daniel the first day he prayed, but was held up for twenty-one days. The enemy was trying to cause a pattern interruption, to the plans of God coming forth. Daniel continued to press in, pray, and intercede for Gods' plans to come forth.

It's important to remember there is a spiritual war going on in the heavens. Paul tells us in Ephesians 6:12:

> *"We wrestle not against flesh and blood, but against principalities, against the rulers of the darkness of this age, against spiritual hosts of wickedness in the heavenly places."*

If the enemy can't steal your provision, he will do everything to delay it (John 10:10). Satan knows if he can get you to lose hope and become discouraged it may cause you to get frustrated and give up.

If you are experiencing a pattern interruption, don't allow frustration to overwhelm you. This is a time to press into the promises of God. Pull down the strongholds holding up the blessings in your life from manifesting in their proper season. Take inventory and close the doors in your life that may be giving the enemy legal access into your life. Discerning when and where the enemy has held up avenues of finances in your life will give you clarity and authority to demand a greater increase for pain and suffering. As you press in and stay grounded in the Word of God, the Lord will give you the strategy you need to counter attack what the enemy is trying to delay in your life.

> *"A poverty mindset knowingly or unknowingly will sabotage a person's destiny at some point if not dealt with."*

The Poverty Mindset

In order to successfully emerge in this next season, we must rid ourselves of the poverty mindset. We discussed in the beginning of the chapter. Mindsets affect the way we view God, the world, and ourselves. A poverty mindset knowingly or unknowingly will sabotage a person's destiny at some point if not dealt with. Poverty makes a person always feel a sense of lack, and unworthiness. If you struggle with a poverty mindset, it will affect the way you handle provision.

The poverty mindset is tied to an orphan spirit. One of the main tactics of the orphan spirit is to cause a person to question their standing as a son and daughter of God. When we don't see ourselves as accepted sons and daughters, we'll be incapable of receiving the inheritance or financial emergence God has ordained for us (Ephesians 1:6). Colossians 1:12 says:

> *"Giving thanks to the Father, who has qualified you to share in the inheritance of the that belongs to His people, who live in the light."*

When it comes to the Father, there is never any lack. He is always willing to give us more than enough if we allow Him. Our life should overflow in every area—including finances.

It's time to shift our mindsets from lack to, more than enough. We are transformed by the renewing of our minds according to the Word of God (Romans 12:2). Contrary to religion, it does not glorify God seeing His sons and daughters living in lack or begging. That's a false humility. We were never called to be beggars. As sons and daughters of the Most High, we are royalty (1 Peter 2:9). Having royalty in our blood allows us to use our authority in Christ to gain access to what we need. If we instead operate in a poverty mindset, it will hinder the provision and blessings the Father desires to place in your life in this season.

> *"When it comes to the Father, there is never any lack. He is always willing to give us more than enough if we allow Him."*

A new economy is coming into your life as you begin to emerge. Supernatural provision will meet you where you're willing to step. Obedience will be the key to unlocking next level finances. Don't allow fear and the poverty mindset to sabotage your future.

God is a Giver

"For God so loved the world, that He gave His only begotten Son, that whoever believes in Him shall not perish, but have eternal life."

John 3:16

Meditating on the characteristics of God while you emerge is vital. It's easy to become so accustomed to receiving, that we stop looking like Jesus. In the book of John, there is a story about Mary from Bethany. She was radically touched by Jesus and wanted to pour out her affection on Him. Mary brought an alabaster box that was equivalent to a year's wages and poured it out on the feet of Jesus as an act of worship.

> *"Part of the devil's continual judgment on earth is watching believers transform into the image of God. It's the very image he wanted to be like."*

In that moment, Judas speaks up and objects to what occurred. Judas wasn't only coming against the act; he became an obstacle that resisted her moment to look like Jesus. The devil cannot stand for sons to look like Jesus. Part of the devil's continual judgment on earth is watching believers transform into the image of God. It's the very image he wanted to be like. As your finances emerge, you must possess a heart to advance the Kingdom. You advance the Kingdom by sowing into the lives around you or the ministries that continuously feed you along the way. One of the greatest fights against believers is looking like Jesus in our giving. If we operate in a poverty mindset, it will shut the flow of provision off in our lives.

God is a giver. In your emerging process don't become just a receiver, but also be a giver. It's imperative to remember the biblical principle of reaping and sowing. Galatians 6:7 says, *"Don't be misled; you cannot mock the justice of God. You will always harvest what you plant."* When we give, no matter the capacity it's planting seed to bring forth a harvest in your life. What kind of a harvest do you want?

When your provision begins to flow freely, do not hold tightly to it. The more you give and sow; it opens the gateway for God to bless you. As you give freely and from a pure heart, God will multiply what's in your hand to be more than you could ever imagine (Ephesians 3:20). When we come to the realization all we have is His, we will freely give as He gave to us (Romans 8:32).

Emerging As A Prophetic People

"In the last days, God says, I will pour out my Spirit on all people. Your sons and daughters will prophesy, your young men will see visions, your old men will dream dreams. Even on my servants, both men and women, I will pour out my Spirit in those days, and they will prophesy. I will show wonders in the heavens above and signs on the earth below, blood and fire and billows of smoke. The sun will be turned to darkness and the moon to blood before the coming of the great and glorious day of the Lord. And everyone who calls on the name of the Lord will be saved."

-Acts 2:17-21

"Follow the way of love and eagerly desire gifts of the Spirit, especially prophecy. For anyone who speaks in a tongue does not speak to people but to God. Indeed, no one understands them; they utter mysteries by the Spirit. But the one who prophesies speaks to people for their strengthening, encouraging and comfort. Anyone who speaks in a tongue edifies themselves, but the one who prophesies edifies the church. I would like every one of you to speak in tongues, but I would rather have you prophesy. The one who

> *prophesies is greater than the one who speaks in tongue] unless someone interprets, so that the church may be edified."*
>
> -1 Corinthians 14:1-5
>
> *"From the tribe of Issachar, there were 200 leaders of the tribe with their relatives. All these men understood the signs of the times and knew the best course for Israel to take."*
>
> 1 Chronicles 12:32

Pouring Out His Spirit

In Joel 2 and Acts 2 we read that in the last days God will pour out His Spirit on all flesh. The purpose of the outpouring of His Spirit is to awaken those who are "sleeping" and to display the fullness of God. When the Father pours out His Spirit many will begin to dream, see visions, and prophesy. As the Body of Christ and sons and daughters, it's time we awaken and step into the fullness of the destiny God has placed within us. Like never before, God is pouring out His Spirit in an unprecedented measure. We are living in a time where the earth will be filled with knowledge of the glory of the Lord (Habakkuk 2:14). All of creation is waiting for the sons and daughters to arise. We are called oaks of righteousness, planted by the Lord meant to display His splendor (Isaiah 61:3).

In order for us to display His glory and splendor in our lives, we have to fully walk in what the Father intended for us. As a whole, the Body of Christ has not been walking and functioning in how God purposed it. The focus in the Church has been on who's in the pulpit, which has taken the focus off those in the pews. The Body is made up of many parts (1 Corinthians 12:12). The five-fold ministry was established to help equip the body to walk in the fullness as a Church and as sons and daughters (Ephesians 4:11-12).

The Prophetic

If you've noticed in the last few years there has been a rise in understanding the prophetic, prophets, and prophecy. This is strategic. Many may feel like it's a new concept, but really it's going back to the foundation. As a believer we all have the capacity to walk in a measure of the prophetic, and to prophesy. You do not have to be a prophet to prophesy. A

> *"As prophetic people, we are carriers of the glory of God. Everywhere we go, we are mandated to release the DNA of heaven, and the heart of the Father."*

prophet is a five-fold office that functions with a certain authority and jurisdiction.

What does it mean to prophesy as a believer? In its simplest definition, it's hearing what Jesus is saying, and speaking it out. Jesus modeled this for us. In John 5:19 Jesus said, "*Very truly I tell you, the Son can do nothing by himself; he can only do what he sees his Father doing.*" To be a prophetic people we must learn to walk, and be led by the Spirit. Revelation 19:10 tells us, "*The Spirit of prophecy is the testimony of Jesus.*" When we begin to prophesy, we release what Jesus is doing. It unlocks faith, enabling people to step into it and allow the word to work in their lives.

The Apostle Paul tells us that we should earnestly seek after the gifts of the Spirit, especially to prophesy. The gift of prophesy is powerful. It has the ability to shift a person's life. The purpose of prophecy is to strengthen, encourage, and comfort (1 Corinthians 14:3). The more we exercise our gift the stronger it will grow. We all can prophesy according to the measure of faith we posses (Romans 12:6). Many people long to know and hear what the Father is saying about them and their situation. We live in a time where there is so much negativity and death. One word from the Father can change anything. The power of life and death is released when we speak. As a prophetic people we carry the Word of the Lord to shift lives, regions, and nations.

The function to prophesy helps us partner with heaven. We are conduits for heaven to be released. As a prophetic people it's our responsibility to advance the Kingdom of God. The Word of God says, *"The Kingdom of Heaven has been forcefully advancing, and the violent take it by force* "(Matthew 11:12). There is a new remnant emerging to release a new facet of the Kingdom of God. We can help establish the Kingdom of God in a greater measure by what we prophesy.

The ability to prophesy gives us the power to create and establish. We see an example of this in Genesis 1. God created and established the heavens, earth, and man by the words He spoke. As a prophetic people we have the ability create, shift, and establish heaven here on earth. That means if something on earth doesn't match the blueprint of heaven, we have the capability to prophesy until it matches what heaven intended for it. In this era, we're going to see a greater rise in creative miracles because we're going to understand the power of creating with the Father. Remember, prophesying is seeing and hearing what the Father is doing, and then speaking it into existence.

The Supernatural

In this era, we're going to begin to see the rise of the Daniels and Josephs. God is placing an emphasis on those who dream and see in the Spirit. As a prophetic people, we have to take back the power of the supernatural. We have allowed the enemy to pervert and counterfeit the supernatural. This generation is mesmerized by the supernatural and demonic. Their hunger for the supernatural has led them to seek after new age practices and false prophetic means because the Church has remained silent.

Throughout the Bible we can see from the Old Testament to the New Testament, the supernatural was something that defined the Israelites and the Church of Acts. Dreams, visions, seeing angels, seeing into the spirit realm, etc. are a part of our make up as a prophetic people. There has been so much emphasis on the demonic realm that we tend to fixate on only seeing the demonic. Just as we can prophesy according to our faith, we see according to our faith. What are you placing your faith in to see?

In this era, the dreamers and seers are emerging. This may seem like a new concept, but dreamers, seers, and those who interpret dreams were a big part of the Bible. A seer is someone who gains revelation through seeing in the spiritual realm through dreams, visions, and through all five senses. The enemy has attempted to shut down this gifting in many through means of fear, nightmares, and rejection from those around them. He's done this because the ability to see into the spiritual realm and discern what is going on is key right now in the earth. Two of the greatest seers of the Bible were Daniel and Joseph. God not only wants to use this gift in the Church, but also wants to use it outside of walls of the Church.

He desires to place the Daniels and Josephs in the marketplace and in governmental positions to turn the hearts of leaders and change the destiny of nations. God will often speak to leaders and rulers through dreams, and the Daniels and Josephs are needed to bring the interpretations. God is going to raise up dreamers that will change the destiny of a nation, because of a dream. He will use seers to expose the plans of the enemy.

As a prophetic people we have a mandate and commission to infiltrate every fiber and level of society and government. We must stop fearing the culture around us, it was never meant for us to stay within the confines of a church building. Transformation to our culture will never come if we're unwilling take over every area of society. Prophetic teacher, Lance Wallnau, teaches there are seven mountains of influence we as a prophetic people need to rule in. The mountains are business, government, media, arts and entertainment, education, family, and religion. We are called to rule and reign in every area of society. It's time to take back what is ours.

The Issachar Anointing

Along with the seer anointing being released, the Issachar anointing is being poured out in our time in a greater measure. In 1 Chronicles 12 we read about the Issachar tribe who were one of the twelve tribes of Judah. They were made up of 200 leaders. This tribe was distinguished for their ability to understand and discern the times, signs, and seasons of their era. Like the tribe of Issachar, we must be sensitive to the Spirit being able to discern and knowing what's going on in the season.

Ecclesisastes 3:1-4 says:

> *"There is a time for everything, and a season for every activity under the heavens, a time to be born, and a time to die, and time to plant and a time to uproot, a time to kill and a time to heal, a time to tear down and time to build, a time to weep and a time to laugh, a time to mourn and a time to dance."*

As a prophetic people we must know the times and seasons. If we're unable to distinguish the timing of God, we'll try the right thing in the wrong timing. Not knowing the times and seasons can cause delay and frustration on a personal level and Church level.

To move prophetically as a people, we must tune our ears and eyes to hear what the Spirit of God is saying in this hour. When God speaks, it's our responsibility to release it in the earth to build, uproot, tear down, or repair. God desires to release a new era, but will only do it if you're willing to partner with Him. Jesus never released or did anything without partnering with the Father. It's time to partner with the Father and emerge!

Made in the USA
Middletown, DE
15 February 2017